Which Has More?

Daisy Allyn

INFOMAX COMMON CORE READERS

Rosen Classroom™

New York

Published in 2013 by The Rosen Publishing Group, Inc.
29 East 21st Street, New York, NY 10010

Book Design: Michael Harmon

Photo Credits: Cover Africa Studio/Shutterstock.com; pp. 5, 9, 13 (spoon) Pefkos/Shutterstock.com; pp. 5, 7, 11, 15 (cup) Alexandr Vlassyuk/Shutterstock.com; p. 7 (jug) Ljupco Smokovski/Shutterstock.com; p. 9 (pot) Kamira/Shutterstock.com; p. 11 (sink) © iStockphoto.com/izusek; p. 13 (tub) © iStockphoto.com/LockieCurrie; p. 15 (pool) Alfgar/Shutterstock.com.

ISBN: 978-1-4488-8884-9
6-pack ISBN: 978-1-4488-8885-6

Manufactured in the United States of America

CPSIA Compliance Information: Batch #WS12RC: For further information contact Rosen Publishing, New York, New York at 1-800-237-9932.

Word Count: 30

Contents

The cup has more water.

The jug has more water.

The pot has more water.

The sink has more water.

The tub has more water.

The pool has more water.

Words to Know

cup

jug

pool

pot

sink

tub

Index